They lie to us

What is lie? Why do people lie? What are types of lying? Combination of truth and untruth as way to manipulate, lie and natural selection, lie in politics – all of this and even more is waiting for you inside this book.

by Anton Kravtsov and Sergey Galan

Table of Contents

Introduction

Dr. House: «Everybody lies. »

Lies surround us everywhere. We deal with it so often that we barely noticing people lying to us. You lie to your boss that you are busy, he in response lies to you that there is no money for pay rise, wife lies about her feelings, and you lie to her about men-only meeting, your son lies about test results, even your best friend lies about your not- so-dusty appearance. Just like an arrogant character from a wide known TV show said: "Everybody lies". Today I decided to puzzle out why do people try to fool you and how crucial it can be in terms of your personal interests.

LIE – what is it?

First of all, let`s find out what is lie. If swindler promises to give your money back, knowing that he would not do it, it is a **LIE**. If you say to him, that you do not have any spare money, but in fact you do, it is a **LIE**. From another side, if that swindler promises to return your money, and he intended to do so, it is not a lie. Or if his friend, that was a person, who came up with the idea of scam, indeed responsible for everything, it is also not a lie. As you see, lying can be different. And it is not always bad. Sometimes lying may be done for the best. So how should we define lie?

Lie – it is wittingly untrue statement. In another words, it is an attempt to seed wrong knowledge in another person`s head. This attempt can be successful (if subject believed) or not (if subject realized getting fooled).

Why do people try to plague wittingly **UNTRUE** information into others? Everything is pretty easy. Lie – it is a powerful way to influence other people in society.

With the help of lying it is possible to **CHANGE PERSONAL VIEWS**, that manage people's decisions. It means that lie – it is an instrument of manipulation that may be used for gaining some profit.

What is profit here? **PROFIT** – it is an income in the form of any resource. Swindler deceives to get resource – money. Son doesn`t want to tell about an F-mark, because he wants you to buy a video game console or avoid getting punished (in this way he gets negative income). Friend tells that you look awesome, because he doesn`t want to aggravate your relationships (it would be a negative income). Girl lies about periods as she doesn`t want to waste her time on men, in which she is not interested. In another words, **LIE** – it is a method of wasting resources in the most beneficial way. For bad purposes? Not necessarily!

You may lie for **YOUR OWN** interests, and also for **OTHERS** interests. For example, when person confesses in crime he didn`t commit (to cover someone). Or when man makes expensive gifts to his beloved and tells that he doesn`t need gift in return. Or, when mother tells about scary monsters to make her child behave. In all this situations people act for sake of OTHERS benefit, so you can misinform not only for yourself!

However, nearly every time, in such cases behind others benefit your own benefit is hiding (masterfully sometimes). Convicted will get plenty of respect during his imprisonment and some help after. Girlfriend attitude to her man will improve. Child will grow healthy and that is exactly what his mother needs. Concluding all this, we can differ two main reasons of lying.

Reasons of lying:

—Personal benefit

—Others benefit

As you can see, reason will totally determine attitude to lying in society. If you lie for your personal benefit, it is bad. If you lie for others benefit, it is closely always good. Why closely? Imagine yourself, that you cheat for your son`s income. Technically it is not for your personal benefit, but people will not accept it, because this action is not profitable for developing of society. From the other point of view, if you will listen to yourself, described situation appears to be slightly better, than cheating to increase personal earnings. That is why people used to think that lying for yourself = bad, for others = good.

Why do people more comfortable with lying for others? Because lying for yourself – it is demonstration of egoism, which always weakens relationships between people in community, that is bad for it. Oppositely, lying for others – it is an act of altruism, which makes relationships in community stronger. If girl accidentally had broken shop-window, and you covered her in front of cops, most are going to say it is good. But if you did that and began to lie, that it wasn`t you, most will admit it is bad. Everything is elementary: judging depends on aiming of your lying.

In 99% of situations people LIE FOR SAKE OF OWN PROFIT! That is why in 99% cases people condemn lying. That is why you always hear that lying it is bad. In Christianity lie – it is an invention of devil. If closely every time lying badly affects relationships in society, it easier and better to say straight off **LYING – IT IS BAD**, instead of explain like I do right now.

Remember, always, when lying appears there is someone`s personal interest. In most cases we are speaking about direct profit of person that lies. Due to lying he gets necessary resource, that often gets lost by object of lie. For instance, when guy promises marriage to a girl just to spend a night with her, he gets self-satisfaction (increases his self-evaluation). On the other hand, girl loses confidence in her internal world (she might think that something wrong with her, if people needs her for sex only). And I am not even talking about more ordinary situations, in which people lie for money, time or comfort.

There is, of course, more vivid lie. Lie, in which it is not so obvious to spot someone`s profit. But it always presents. For example, person makes something very helpful for other people, but when they starting to speak well about him, he for some reasons disagrees with them. He tells (lies actually) that he is worse than he is indeed. i.e. he is afraid of looking clean-living and honest. Sometimes good people are trying to look worse than they are. Looking bad is more comfortable for them. This feature is inherited in really good people (shit people do quite the opposite). So who wins in such unusual case of lying?

He lies that he is worse than he really is. That is not true. So what is the point in such deception? If people think that he worse than he is indeed, it will be bad for him. Or not?

He avoids other people think that he makes good just for personal purposes (to seem good person, show off). But he makes it for other`s success (even when it is not profitable for him). Contradiction appears, that can be solved only by lowering yourself. And in the end it produces a profit to our character, because such a thing rises him even higher in the eyes of others. Modesty attracts.

Types of lie

As you already noticed, lying may has various forms depending on practicability. I differ types of lying such as:

—Direct lie

—Distortion of information

—Hiding some information

Direct lie – it is a type of lying, when you completely change the information. For instance, if you ask someone to borrow you some cash until salary, but you do not have a job. You DIRECTLY changed the fact of having job. Said you have it, but you have not. You did it only for getting money.

Distortion – it is a type of lying, when you replace only some piece of information. If you ask to borrow until salary, but you are currently on probation and you get nothing, it is a distortion. You DISTORTED the fact of getting salary. Yes, you have a job (you did not lie directly), but you will not get any money (it is a distortion). And again you did it only for getting money.

Hiding – that is a variant of passive lying, when you get the right result by not doing something. For instance, you are as usual asking your neighbor to borrow money, but this time you are hiding the fact of getting fired. Yes, you have not done any active actions to fool your neighbor. You just did not give the full information. But it was for personal profit.

Direct lying and distortion needs ACTIVE actions (means you have to do something), hiding instead needs PASSIVE actions (means you have to just keep silent, and person will summarize just like you want independently). Now you see that you do not necessarily need to say something in order to lie (active actions). You can just remain silent for getting profit.

Hiding, by the way, commonly used for other people`s interests. Say me why young soldier needs to know everything about all scary things that he will face during war? Or, for example, for sake of what patient have to know that five similar operations before were failed, if he needs it anyway? It will only make him nervous. That is why wise people keep silent. But not for themselves, but for others.

Lie is unique way of changing information. You don`t even need to say something to use it. You can just create false view on reality by appropriate actions or even gestures. And often it will be more effective than direct verbal lying. For example, when Rothschilds after Napoleon`s losing bought the whole England they did not tell: 'Napoleon already won and now he will destroy England, so you should sell British as fast as possible'. No. Instead of this he appeared in pretty mirthless mood at stoke exchange in the morning and begun defiantly sell British companies. All players decided that he already know about Napoleon`s victory (if he behaves so). Rothschild fooled all other players and they started to sell British companies in a big hurry, crashing the market. In a very same moment Rothschild`s accomplices bought up companies ridiculously cheap. It was non-verbal deception. Rothschild remained silent. But his mimics and actions distorted the truth in a way he wanted. That is exactly how (by lying) the world biggest capital was born.

White lie

We talked about types of lie (direct, distortion, hiding). But it is common categories, in which there could be some subtypes. And white lie it is one of such subtypes that we already dealt with.

White lie – it is a misinformation of other people for someone else`s interests. For example, when you support a wimp, telling him he looks good. Or, when you say to your fat sister that she is very gorgeous. Most of the time, if you say the truth, nothing good will happen: person will feel worse. That is the reason you lie. You lie for other people`s interests.

Another sample of such lying is stories for kids, that allow you to fool kids for their benefit.

LIE VS TRUTH

But wait, is it not possible to achieve goals by truth? It is, though range of abilities is smaller. Yes, truth – it is a way to influence people`s actions. Lie either. But first method is **social** (consider interests of all), and second is **biological** (based on instincts). Strictly speaking, **truth + lie** gives person more abilities for manipulation of people around in sake of personal benefit. Yes, it is bad from society`s point of view, but if you are real animal, which thinks only from its own egoistical point of view, you do not care about others. In this case, you get more powerful tool of manipulation.

The biggest paradox for me is that lie – it is an intelligent behavior, but when you use it for personal interests – it is an animal behavior. And now we have pretty comical situation: intellect serves for animal instincts of human! It sounds weird only at first glance. If you take thoughts, you will find out that our brain was created for solving biological tasks: **food, sex and dominance!**

Despite Rothschilds have unlimited amount of money (they can print them as much as they want), they still continue to cheat. Why? After all they have enough food (money) to feed lots of countries, not only for their own families. They do not have lack of authority (dominance): they have influence on all main world`s governments. Why they reaching for more? It is not intelligently! Because, my dear friend, tasks of getting food, sex and dominance are biological. They ruled by animal instinct, not by intellect. That is why it is always not enough! That is why not intelligently! Because intellect does not take a part in it. Same situation with love. Questions of reproduction are vital, so nature entrusted them to instincts instead of intellect. Due to this your decisions are so intelligently, intellect can`t explain why you love this shitass.

Natural selection

So, may be **lie for personal benefit – it is good?** If we even have it written in our instincts, may be it is important. It can`t be done by mistake. YES. Everything is right: not by mistake. It is written in genes of all animals to make them fight for limited resources, finding out who is the best. It is called **natural selection**.

Lying for personal profit – it is a way to win in natural selection. The point is simple: **win no matter how**! Prove you are the best. But animal instincts not really fit humans, because we`ve got intellect and ability to act intelligently. In the result of natural selection survived communities and people that were more social and could exist in a massive social groups. These people conquered and destroyed weaker communities and weaker people. Needful condition for that was intelligent social behavior: share food, cooperate for better result, not killing each other for nothing etc. For that **intellect** was created. Yes, it is also biological tasks, but to solve them better it was important to study how to behave at least partially intelligently with other people (be honest, cooperate, hide aggression). Differently speaking, it was necessary to suppress greater part of biological for developing social. And that caused advantage in natural selection.

However, process of «suppressing» very long and stretched out for millions years of evolution as living creatures can`t change shortly. In result we`ve got set of biological (animal) and social (intelligent) in ourselves. And besides at this moment animal part in humans presented more than intelligent, because intellect more often serves to animal instincts, not vice versa. We already have learned not to kill another human for food or mate (suppressed some animal habits), but we still haven`t learned to stop, when there is plenty of food, mates and power. We always want more. And it completely corresponds to animal behavior.

Social(common) interests must be more important than egoistical(personal) to make society develop and to share gain between all members. In this case nearer partnership between people is possible and as a result bigger income from such cooperation. But for that you have to suppress animal habits and pull out all intellectual, means not to lie for personal benefit. And for every animal it is hard to reject its initial nature. That is the main problem…

Political correctness

In narrow sense it is a prohibition of using phrases that are considered to be abusive for certain social groups divided by race, nationality, sex, age, religion or sexual orientation. Actually you distort information for personal benefit, because if you say the truth in most direct form, it will make it more difficult to get the right result from opponent. Commonly used by professional politics as for them every voter counts (despite skin color, religion, age etc.).

Why do politics call their enemies «**Partners**»? It is the most obvious example of lying for sake of personal interests, that named political correctness. If you call them enemies, you will have only one choice – to fight them. And you will not be able to negotiate with them.

To make it more clear, think why boy tells girl «about love», «about how beautiful she is», «about how he likes her as personality». Why he just doesn`t tell the truth «about how pleasurable she can be», «about how cool her breasts», «that he dreams to be in one bed with her». Guy demonstrate political correctness, because if he tells the truth, then the girl will not leave him any chances. In fact, guy forced to be politically correct. Same thing in politics. We better not to say something like: «*our enemies, @$!Q#, kicked our asses in 1991 and forced to pay tribute, but now we are done*». Such truth leads to bad result. You better say that «*socio-economic conditions changed and now we should review old agreements with our partners*» etc.

In which situations serious politic may tell the truth in no uncertain terms? In situations, when he has ability to stand by his words! If he has no power and independency for that, he should very carefully express your thoughts, because all words can be used against speaker.

Conclusion

Dear reader, I hope that I managed to give you the useful information. Talking about practice, I don`t recommend to anyone acutely react to lie. It is better to perceive it like something natural as it appeared for some reason, and in nature nothing happens without reason. Wise people more often adapt to environment and don`t try to change it. So you should take it easy and use lie like an instrument, consequences of using which depends on person that appliAes it.

They lie to us

Author:
Anton Kravtsov
Translator/editor:
Sergey
Galagan